THE WRITING PROMPT BOOK FOR AWESOME (AND AWESOMELY F'ED-UP) PEOPLE

Written by: CJ Carr

(with contributions from Jamie Taperek)

What's the most annoying thing that's recently became
popular on the internet? Why do you hate it?

_____

_____

_____

_____

_____

_____

_____

_____

_____

_____

_____

_____

_____

_____

Write the greatest dead baby joke ever conceived by
mankind.

_____

_____

_____

_____

_____

_____

_____

You fucked your best friend's mom. How do you break
it to them that you're their new step-parent?

_____

_____

_____

_____

_____

_____

_____

What is the most unproductive thing that you love to
do and just can't stop doing, even though it's
unproductive AF?

_____

_____

_____

_____

_____

_____

_____

_____

_____

_____

_____

_____

_____

_____

_____

You somehow become the master of the Great Lord
Cthulhu. How do you use his power that's now at your
will?

_____

_____

_____

_____

_____

_____

_____

_____

_____

_____

_____

_____

_____

Google your full name. Write a summary of the first
real article with someone (who isn't you) with your
name.

_____

_____

_____

_____

_____

_____

_____

Why did you decide to buy this book? Will you buy my
other book(s)? You totally should.

_____

_____

_____

_____

_____

_____

_____

You're trapped in an early 1900's mental ward. Plot
your escape.

_____

_____

_____

_____

_____

_____

_____

_____

_____

_____

_____

_____

_____

Finish this sentence: "I'm gonna kill you, you goat-raping, she-devil, bitch of a whore's ass! I'll never forgive you for . . ."

_____

_____

_____

_____

_____

_____

_____

So, did he cum or what?

_____

_____

_____

_____

_____

_____

_____

For the first time in history, REAL artificial
intelligence is born. How does the inevitable global
takeover happen, and how long from the birth of the
this real A.I. does it take to start the onslaught
and genocide of the human race?

_____

_____

_____

_____

_____

_____

_____

_____

_____

_____

_____

_____

You have sex on the beach. The woman you're with gets
a grain of sand in her vagina and something MAGICAL
happens. What does that magical grain of sand turn
into?

_____

_____

_____

_____

_____

_____

_____

Give the city you live in a new name that reflects
the shittyness of it. Why that name?

_____

_____

_____

_____

_____

_____

Write a Christmas song about how Santa is bringing STD's to all the good little girls and boys this year.

_____

_____

_____

_____

_____

_____

_____

_____

_____

_____

_____

_____

_____

_____

DC/Marvel/Indie? Discuss.

_____

_____

_____

_____

_____

_____

_____

_____

_____

_____

_____

_____

_____

_____

_____

_____

You are an alien that is in disguise among the
humans. Describe a typical day in your life as this
secret spy living in a weird world.

_____

_____

_____

_____

_____

_____

_____

_____

_____

_____

_____

_____

_____

_____

What is the meaning of life? Be deep (like your mom).

_____

_____

_____

_____

_____

_____

_____

_____

_____

_____

_____

_____

_____

_____

If you knew you were going to be trapped on an island but could only bring three things (besides the clothes you are wearing), what would they be? It can't be anything technological, including smartphones or vibrators.

_____

_____

_____

_____

_____

_____

What's the stupidest question you've ever heard someone ask?

_____

_____

_____

_____

_____

_____

Write a love story of a frog and a princess who has
weird sexual feelings for frogs.

_____

_____

_____

_____

_____

_____

_____

_____

_____

_____

_____

_____

_____

_____

_____

Time travelers come back to the past and say that
they need to kill you in order to save the entire
world. What the fuck did you do in order to have
people sent back in time to kill you?

_____

_____

_____

_____

_____

_____

Chimi-fucking-chongas or tacos?

_____

_____

_____

_____

_____

_____

_____

What is your most attractive quality? How can you convince people of this without sounding like an arrogant d-bag?

_____

_____

_____

_____

_____

_____

_____

_____

_____

_____

_____

_____

_____

_____

Answer why the sky is blue in the most illogical way
you can imagine. Something like a paranoid
schizophrenic might say, perhaps?

_____

_____

_____

_____

_____

_____

Who pushes your buttons the easiest and most? What
buttons can they push that just fucking irks you?

_____

_____

_____

_____

_____

_____

You work at an intergalactic animal shelter. You are the only human most of the clients and staff have ever seen. They keep thinking you are an escaped pet. Explain to them how humans aren't just balding bipedal apes and you are nobodies pet.

_____

_____

_____

_____

_____

_____

_____

_____

_____

_____

_____

_____

_____

_____

Analyze the dream you had this morning in as much
detail as you can. If you don't remember it, analyze
the last dream that you can vividly remember.
Describe every detail and symbolic meaning that you
can muster.

_____

_____

_____

_____

_____

_____

_____

_____

_____

_____

_____

_____

_____

List eight ridiculous names for a boat.

_____

_____

_____

_____

_____

_____

_____

You are your favorite food and sentient at that.
Describe your last thoughts as someone is about to
eat you.

_____

_____

_____

_____

_____

_____

_____

You are given a magical chalk and everything you draw comes to life. The problem is that you suck total ass at drawing. What happens when the stick figures and other horrible art you draw comes to life?

_____

_____

_____

_____

_____

_____

_____

_____

_____

_____

_____

_____

_____

When life gives you lemons, what the fuck do you do?

_____

_____

_____

_____

_____

_____

If your entire life up to this point could only be
described by one color, what would it be and why?

_____

_____

_____

_____

_____

_____

_____

If you have tattoos, what's your most meaningful one?
Why is it special to you? If you don't have any
tattoos, what would you get, assuming that you **had** to
get one?

_____

_____

_____

_____

_____

_____

_____

_____

_____

_____

_____

_____

_____

After years of having to deal with being just a lowly member of a pirate crew, you finally have your own ship and crew of which you are the captain. Your sister, however, demands that you make her husband, Jerry, your first-mate. Jerry is a TOTAL dick and you've hated him since the day you met him, but you love your sister and you take him on anyway. Make a list of horrible pirate duties for Jerry to check off so you can make his dick-being life suck.

_____

_____

_____

_____

_____

_____

_____

_____

_____

_____

_____

Write a journal entry as if you're pretty sure you're going to be murdered in the next couple of days but no one believes you.

_____

_____

_____

_____

_____

_____

_____

_____

_____

_____

_____

_____

_____

_____

You walk down your street and see some kid is sitting
on the sidewalk crying in its own shit. How do you
tell it to grow the fuck up and stop shitting itself?

_____

_____

_____

_____

_____

_____

You masturbate for the first time and something
magical comes out of your genitals. What is it?

_____

_____

_____

_____

_____

_____

You give yourself a pep talk in the mirror. Your
reflection starts talking back to and (kinda) is
being a TOTAL Debby Downer. What does it tell you?

_____

_____

_____

_____

_____

_____

_____

_____

_____

_____

_____

_____

_____

_____

What is the first thing you would do if you became
super rich out of the blue?

_____

_____

_____

_____

_____

_____

_____

_____

_____

_____

_____

_____

_____

_____

What do you feel is your destiny or utmost mission in life?

_____

_____

_____

_____

_____

_____

_____

_____

_____

_____

_____

_____

_____

_____

If you could be the size of a bug and spy on anyone, who would you spy on and what do you think you would learn?

_____

_____

_____

_____

_____

_____

_____

_____

_____

_____

_____

_____

_____

_____

Finish this sentence: "I would love to change . . ."

_____

_____

_____

_____

_____

_____

_____

Describe the weirdest thing you've ever found in a pocket of an article of clothing that you didn't know was there.

_____

_____

_____

_____

_____

_____

_____

You have your head cryogenically frozen after you die and 1,000 years in the future you are (somehow) brought back to life. What is this world like? What are you like now having been previously just a dead, frozen head?

_____

_____

_____

_____

_____

_____

_____

_____

_____

_____

_____

_____

_____

_____

You're in your underwear in front of the entire
class. You aren't dreaming. You really went to school
in just your undies. Realizing this, you also realize
you have to take a super massive shit and you know
you won't even make it to the classroom door.
Describe what happens next.

_____

_____

_____

_____

_____

_____

_____

_____

_____

_____

_____

_____

_____

What's your lucky number? Why is it your lucky number?

_____

_____

_____

_____

_____

_____

What's your go-to for relieving stress?

_____

_____

_____

_____

_____

_____

_____

Your best friend (or significant other) is talking
about killing themselves. Talk them out of it by
telling them how much they have to live for, etc.

_____

_____

_____

_____

_____

_____

_____

_____

_____

_____

_____

_____

_____

_____

Jerry doesn't do his job of swabbing the poop decks right. Ever. 'Cause he's a SUPER dick. In song form, explain to him how it's done correctly.

_____

_____

_____

_____

_____

_____

_____

_____

_____

_____

_____

_____

_____

_____

If someone was willing to give you a large sum of
money to have sex with them, but they have an STD,
what STD's would you be ok with, and what would your
lowest amount be to have sex with them?

_____

_____

_____

_____

_____

_____

Look up the literal meaning of your full name. Does
it sound like you? If it doesn't, describe a person
you know who it does sound like.

_____

_____

_____

_____

_____

_____

_____

Describe the last movie you saw (in detail) to someone who has been blind all of their life.

_____

_____

_____

_____

_____

_____

_____

_____

_____

_____

_____

_____

_____

_____

Natalie Portman with a penis or Ryan Gosling with a
vagina? Explain your choice.

_____

_____

_____

_____

_____

_____

_____

If you do drugs, what's your drug of choice and why?
If you don't do drugs, what would you be willing to
try?

_____

_____

_____

_____

_____

_____

What's your preferred way to die? Explain (in great
length) why and how you think you actually will end
up dying.

_____

_____

_____

_____

_____

_____

_____

_____

_____

_____

_____

_____

_____

_____

You can bring back one person from the dead for 24
hours. Who do you bring back, and how do you spend
those 24 hours with them?

_____

_____

_____

_____

_____

_____

_____

_____

_____

_____

_____

_____

_____

_____

_____

You find out that the universal force of gravity is
sentient and starts talking to you. What does it say?

_____

_____

_____

_____

_____

_____

_____

Why are so many people stupid, IYO?

_____

_____

_____

_____

_____

_____

_____

Rewrite the 10 Commandments to accommodate how (a lot of) Christians **really** act.

_____

_____

_____

_____

_____

_____

_____

_____

_____

_____

_____

_____

_____

_____

Begin a great story of the world's greatest hero (super or non-super) who (as the story begins) is dealing with IBS (Irritable Bowel Syndrome).

_____

_____

_____

_____

_____

_____

_____

_____

_____

_____

_____

_____

_____

_____

It's bring your daughter to work day, but you work in
the porn industry. Show your daughter around the set
and explain to her what your job entails.

_____

_____

_____

_____

_____

_____

_____

_____

_____

_____

_____

_____

_____

_____

Finish this sentence: "Diamonds are forever, but so
is . . ."

_____

_____

_____

_____

_____

_____

If you had a pet dragon, what would you name it?
Describe him (or her).

_____

_____

_____

_____

_____

_____

_____

_____

_____

You're immortal and you live countless lifetimes
watching the people you love die. Describe the next
five centuries, century by century.

_____

_____

_____

_____

_____

_____

_____

_____

_____

_____

_____

_____

_____

_____

What's your favorite animal? What's the animal that
you hate the most, assuming you hate any?

_____

_____

_____

_____

_____

_____

_____

_____

_____

_____

_____

_____

_____

You are about to bury a time capsule for future you.
You think it'd be hilarious if you filled it with
really bizarre (current) fad items that you'll forget
by the time you open it in 20 years. What's in it?
Why did the things you put in become forgettable?

_____

_____

_____

_____

_____

_____

_____

_____

_____

_____

_____

_____

_____

What's your five-year plan? Does it include a guy
with old balls?

_____

_____

_____

_____

_____

_____

_____

_____

_____

_____

_____

_____

_____

You're in a sword duel, fighting for your life, and Jerry won't stop asking you (mid-fight) how much treasure you recently plummeted. Because Jerry is your first-mate, the crew's accountant, AND a total dick with no social skills. How do you apologize to the guy you're fighting to the death for Jerrys lack of social grace?

_____

_____

_____

_____

_____

_____

_____

_____

_____

_____

_____

_____

Use your phone's predicting dictionary to write a
story. You can only use words that pop up on the left
or right (not the middle word). Try and make it make
sense, and fill up all the lines on this page.

_____

_____

_____

_____

_____

_____

_____

_____

_____

_____

_____

_____

_____

_____

Where are you right now while writing this? Describe your surroundings in a creative way from someone who's never seen it before.

_____

_____

_____

_____

_____

_____

_____

Do you have insomnia or do you usually get really good sleep? If you do have insomnia, what is it that keeps you up?

_____

_____

_____

_____

_____

_____

_____

If the characters of your all-time favorite fictional
book came to life and appeared in front of you, what
would you say to them?

_____

_____

_____

_____

_____

_____

_____

_____

_____

_____

_____

_____

_____

_____

What was one golden opportunity you were given that
you didn't take? Why didn't you take it? Stupid ass.

_____

_____

_____

_____

_____

_____

_____

_____

_____

_____

_____

_____

_____

_____

You're a knight in medieval Europe. Someone from the year 2016 goes back in time and appears right in front of you. What do you think they are? Describe what they have on them (maybe a phone) as any knight from medieval Europe might.

_____

_____

_____

_____

_____

_____

You move back in with your parents and walk in on them one day having sex. How do they explain that Daddy is only wrestling with Mommy?

_____

_____

_____

_____

_____

Write a legit journal entry for today.

_____

_____

_____

_____

_____

_____

_____

_____

_____

_____

_____

_____

_____

_____

You look outside and notice the zombie apocalypse has officially begun. What. The. Fuck. Do. You. Do?

_____

_____

_____

_____

_____

_____

_____

_____

_____

_____

_____

_____

_____

_____

_____

You are in group therapy for people who have PTSD
from dealing with stupid and douchebag people
everywhere, ALL the time. Introduce yourself and why
you came to the group and what you plan to get out of
it.

_____

_____

_____

_____

_____

_____

_____

_____

_____

_____

_____

_____

Write a quick love story that's both funny and
incredibly tragic.

_____

_____

_____

_____

_____

_____

_____

_____

_____

_____

_____

_____

_____

_____

_____

A gypsy tells you that you're gonna die in 3 days. Do you take your own life, or wait it out and see what happens? What happens if you wait the 3 days? For the sake of this prompt, the gypsy is (unbelievably) accurate.

_____

_____

_____

_____

_____

_____

What's your opinion on Hollywood reboots?

_____

_____

_____

_____

_____

_____

_____

What are three "pipedream" goals for your life you have that people tell you you'll never achieve and that you should just give up?

_____

_____

_____

_____

_____

_____

_____

_____

_____

_____

_____

_____

_____

_____

_____

If you had a superpower (just one), what it would it be? Why that one and what would you do with it?

_____

_____

_____

_____

_____

_____

_____

_____

_____

_____

_____

_____

_____

_____

What do you believe happens when we die?

_____

_____

_____

_____

_____

_____

_____

_____

_____

_____

_____

_____

_____

_____

What's the most fucked-up/weirdest thing you found on
accident when searching for something on the
internet?

_____

_____

_____

_____

_____

_____

_____

_____

_____

_____

_____

_____

_____

You're stuck in a dream and can't wake up. It's an awesome dream, but then stuff keeps happening to try and wake you. Describe this awesome dream and the "subtle" hints you keep getting to snap back awake.

_____

_____

_____

_____

_____

_____

_____

_____

_____

_____

_____

_____

_____

_____

What dead celebrity would you have sex with? Why do you want to fuck dead people? Weirdo.

_____

_____

_____

_____

_____

_____

_____

What's one thing you most regret quitting?

_____

_____

_____

_____

_____

_____

_____

A virus has wiped out all the male humans in the world except for you. The fate of the world rests on your shoulders. The problem is they are big, incredibly gay shoulders. How do you explain to the women, as the world's last man, that you aren't going to help them repopulate the earth? How do they react?

_____

_____

_____

_____

_____

_____

_____

_____

_____

_____

_____

_____

_____

What's the thing you are better at than anyone else?

_____

_____

_____

_____

_____

_____

What's the most complicated "simple" thing in your life?

_____

_____

_____

_____

_____

_____

_____

Create ten adorable and loving characters. Describe
them in a decent amount of detail. Make them fight to
the death and declare one the winner.

_____

_____

_____

_____

_____

_____

_____

_____

_____

_____

_____

_____

_____

_____

You're a news anchor and you decide that the top story won't get your show ratings. You then decide to make one up in an effort to appeal to your viewers and get ratings. Make up your fake news story. Good or bad. Write whatever you think will get the highest ratings.

_____

_____

_____

_____

_____

_____

_____

_____

_____

_____

_____

_____

_____

What's the most current and stressful thing going on
in your life right now? How are you going to fix it?

_____

_____

_____

_____

_____

_____

_____

What was one thing as a child you used to think was
the absolute truth that you were embarrassed to find
out wasn't as a grown-ass adult?

_____

_____

_____

_____

_____

_____

_____

Pick up the closest book near you (besides this one).
Turn to page 53 and write down the first sentence at
the top. Then describe how that sentence explains
your current romantic relationship, or the one you
wish you had. Whichever's more clever-er.

_____

_____

_____

_____

_____

_____

_____

_____

_____

_____

_____

_____

_____

You start to think that the government can read
people's minds so you start wearing a tin-foil hat.
It actually helps, but you see how everyone without a
hat the government is stealing their thoughts. How do
you convince them to wear a tin-foil hat?

_____

_____

_____

_____

_____

_____

_____

_____

_____

_____

_____

_____

_____

_____

If you could consume any food/drink/substance nonstop without any adverse consequences, what would it be and why?

_____

_____

_____

_____

_____

_____

_____

If your life had a musical score to accompany everything you did, what kind of music would it predominantly be? What would your theme song be?

_____

_____

_____

_____

_____

_____

Write a short horror story about someone who is
really bad at killing people and kills them with a
random-ass object of your choosing.

_____

_____

_____

_____

_____

_____

_____

_____

_____

_____

_____

_____

_____

_____

_____

Humans from a parallel world take refuge on our
earth. Now the world is full of doppelgangers. You
run into yours one day. How does that go?

_____

_____

_____

_____

_____

_____

_____

_____

_____

_____

_____

_____

_____

_____

Write the chorus to a love song that describes your romantic life at the moment.

_____

_____

_____

_____

_____

_____

_____

You keep waking up at 11:11 a.m. this week. Your boss says it's a sign you're fired, but what do you think it means?

_____

_____

_____

_____

_____

_____

_____

Write an epic story but start somewhere in the middle of it.

_____

_____

_____

_____

_____

_____

_____

_____

_____

_____

_____

_____

_____

_____

_____

What do you consider an artform that other people
usually don't? What makes it an artform to you?

_____

_____

_____

_____

_____

_____

_____

_____

_____

_____

_____

_____

_____

_____

What's your favorite Mario game of all-time? Why is
it so fucking awesome?

_____

_____

_____

_____

_____

_____

_____

If you were a God of something (e.g. buttered toast),
what would it be? Why that?

_____

_____

_____

_____

_____

_____

_____

_____

Fill up these lines with a script of an adult version
of a children's book.

_____

_____

_____

_____

_____

_____

_____

_____

_____

_____

_____

_____

_____

_____

You've been homeless for the last five years,
sleeping on park benches with nothing to your name
but three dirty winter jackets that you wear in one-
hundred-degree weather. Describe the things you've
had to do in order to survive.

_____

_____

_____

_____

_____

_____

_____

_____

_____

_____

_____

_____

_____

_____

If you owned a research and development company, name
ten things you would research or develop given
unlimited resources and talent.

_____

_____

_____

_____

_____

_____

_____

_____

_____

_____

_____

_____

_____

_____

_____

Write about a time someone lied to you for a super
stupid reason.

_____

_____

_____

_____

_____

_____

_____

_____

_____

_____

_____

_____

_____

_____

Make a list of ten names that are the weirdest pun
names for superhero secret identities you can think
of, and describe their super powers and how it
relates to their real names.

_____

_____

_____

_____

_____

_____

_____

_____

_____

_____

_____

_____

_____

_____

Would you date an ex of yours? If so, why did you
break up in the first place? If not, why wouldn't you
date them?

_____

_____

_____

_____

_____

_____

_____

_____

_____

_____

_____

_____

_____

Create a new adversary for the show "Game of
Thrones." Write a bio of them and how they shake
everything up.

_____

_____

_____

_____

_____

_____

_____

_____

_____

_____

_____

_____

_____

_____

Write a story from a Hollywood action scene that
takes five seconds, but in as much detail and with as
much action as possible.

_____

_____

_____

_____

_____

_____

_____

_____

_____

_____

_____

_____

_____

_____

What's something you find completely logical that
nobody else seems to?

_____

_____

_____

_____

_____

_____

_____

_____

_____

_____

_____

_____

_____

_____

What was the strangest déjà vu experience you've ever had?

_____

_____

_____

_____

_____

_____

_____

_____

_____

_____

_____

_____

_____

_____

If you could only watch one TV show for the rest of
your life, what would it be?

_____

_____

_____

_____

_____

_____

You die and go to Hell but they mix up your personal
Hell with your best friend's. What kind of Hell is
it?

_____

_____

_____

_____

_____

_____

Write the plot of an animated movie that's sure to be the next "Frozen."

_____

_____

_____

_____

_____

_____

_____

_____

_____

_____

_____

_____

_____

_____

What exactly is "nerd culture" to you?

_____

_____

_____

_____

_____

_____

_____

_____

_____

_____

_____

_____

_____

_____

What is the most boring thing in the world to you?
Why is it so fucking boring?

_____

_____

_____

_____

_____

_____

_____

_____

_____

_____

_____

_____

_____

Do you have a recurring nightmare? What is it and
what do you think it means?

_____

_____

_____

_____

_____

_____

_____

_____

_____

_____

_____

_____

_____

_____

Your ship is sinking. Jerry is telling you how brave you are for staying with the ship. Jerry is the BIGGEST dick in the world. FUCK Jerry. Explain to him that he has been promoted to captain and can die while you get on a lifeboat.

_____

_____

_____

_____

_____

_____

_____

_____

_____

_____

_____

_____

_____

What's the one lesson in life you never learn? Why
are you so dumb about learning it?

_____

_____

_____

_____

_____

_____

_____

_____

_____

_____

_____

_____

_____

_____

You are an ancient Greek oracle and an army of
Spartans comes to you to foretell the future as they
head to war with the unbeatable Persian army. What do
you see in your vision?

_____

_____

_____

_____

_____

_____

_____

If you could create (or improve on) a phone app, what
would it be?

_____

_____

_____

_____

_____

_____

_____

Humanity has been extinct for millions of years
(since 2016 CE) and an alien race comes to earth and
excavates our buried remains and culture. Describe
humanity of that time from these alien's perspective.

_____

_____

_____

_____

_____

_____

_____

_____

_____

_____

_____

_____

_____

_____

_____

You live in a world where everything that happens in movies are real. People really die, monsters are real monsters, cities are really destroyed, etc. You are cast in the most destructive movie mankind has ever scripted, and you play the role of the main villain. Describe your last scene of the movie.

_____

_____

_____

_____

_____

_____

_____

If you could somehow obtain just one item throughout all of history, what would it be?

_____

_____

_____

_____

_____

_____

In what way has the internet made you stupid and/or lazy?

_____

_____

_____

_____

_____

_____

_____

_____

_____

_____

_____

_____

_____

_____

What are ten songs you'd have played at your funeral?
Explain your choices.

_____

_____

_____

_____

_____

_____

_____

_____

_____

_____

_____

_____

_____

_____

Write a short story knowing that it'll come true if
you write it. There are rules. 1.) It can't be about
you. 2.) Someone has to die in a pathetic and
embarrassing way. 3.) Raptors.

_____

_____

_____

_____

_____

_____

_____

_____

_____

_____

_____

_____

_____

_____

Write about something fucked-up you did and were
caught for but was totally worth it.

_____

_____

_____

_____

_____

_____

_____

_____

_____

_____

_____

_____

_____

What is your most disturbing sexual fetish? Are you
proud or ashamed of it?

_____

_____

_____

_____

_____

_____

_____

Finish this sentence: "You are the dumbest person
I've ever met. . ."

_____

_____

_____

_____

_____

_____

_____

What's the thing you're most afraid of and why are
you afraid of it?

_____

_____

_____

_____

_____

_____

_____

_____

_____

_____

_____

_____

Let's say—for the sake of this prompt—that Earth itself is a living being. Humans are (to the earth) like bacteria that live inside us. Some make us sick, some help. Let's say for a minute that while some people are like bacteria to the earth, some have more of a white blood cell role. What would these people's jobs be, helping to heal the earth of infections?

_____

_____

_____

_____

_____

_____

_____

_____

_____

_____

_____

_____

_____

You can go back in time to one point in your life (in a *Butterfly Effect* kinda way). Where do you go and what do you change? What is the present like after having changed the past?

_____

_____

_____

_____

_____

_____

_____

_____

_____

_____

_____

_____

_____

You live in a world exactly the same as the one now, but nobody is able to lie about anything. Ever. You go on a blind date. They aren't anything like you were imagining. Introduce yourself and then write the convo you two have after you order dinner at a fancy(ish) restaurant.

_____

_____

_____

_____

_____

_____

_____

_____

_____

_____

_____

_____

You're a young teen. Your step-dad is a molestey,
alcoholic dick-douche. He beat up your mom (on
mother's day), and now you finally gather the gusto
to murder the mother-fucker. How do you do it?

_____

_____

_____

_____

_____

_____

You're Silent Bob and it's the one moment you have
something significant to say to motivate and move
along the plot at the climax of the story. What are
your sage words of advice?

_____

_____

_____

_____

_____

You're out having a good time, drinking with friends. You've only had two beers, but all of a sudden you blackout and wake up in a run-down motel room in the desert. There's probably what is a hooker (more than likely with every STD imaginable) lying in your bed next to you, and there's a giant duffle-bag full of money and another one full of coke. Piece together what might have happened.

_____

_____

_____

_____

_____

_____

_____

_____

_____

_____

_____

_____

_____

_____

Time starts to go backwards and every hour it goes in reverse you become a year younger. What do you do with every hour you have left before you go back to being nothing?

_____

_____

_____

_____

_____

_____

_____

_____

_____

_____

_____

_____

_____

What's the grossest bad habit or quality you have?
Have you ever done it in public? Describe a
situation, if you have.

_____

_____

_____

_____

_____

_____

_____

_____

_____

_____

_____

_____

_____

_____

_____

What's the most hilarious thing that's happened to you during sex? Did it stop you from finishing?

_____

_____

_____

_____

_____

_____

_____

_____

_____

_____

_____

_____

_____

What horrible qualities did your parents pass on to
you? Physical and/or mental.

_____

_____

_____

_____

_____

_____

_____

_____

_____

_____

_____

_____

_____

_____

What was the most significant lesson you learned and actually retained in life?

_____

_____

_____

_____

_____

_____

_____

_____

_____

_____

_____

_____

_____

_____

If you could create a charity, what would it be for?
How would you help people and go about promoting it?

_____

_____

_____

_____

_____

_____

_____

_____

_____

_____

_____

_____

_____

_____

As a child what's something horrible you did that
your parents never found out about? What would you do
if your kid(s) did the same thing?

_____

_____

_____

_____

_____

_____

Are you a tits or an ass, man/woman?

_____

_____

_____

_____

_____

_____

_____

What rituals do you have that could be considered obsessive to the point it's basically OCD?

_____

_____

_____

_____

_____

_____

_____

_____

_____

_____

_____

_____

_____

_____

What's the most peaceful place in the world for you?
The place where you go to relax and/or reflect on
life.

_____

_____

_____

_____

_____

_____

_____

_____

_____

_____

_____

_____

_____

Pick an object in your bedroom. Write a diary entry
from its perspective, being something that's
witnessed you doing some fucked-up shit.

_____

_____

_____

_____

_____

_____

_____

_____

_____

_____

_____

_____

_____

_____

If you could get rid of one emotion (just for you,
personally) forever, what would it be and why?

_____

_____

_____

_____

_____

_____

_____

_____

_____

_____

_____

_____

_____

_____

Describe a time you mentored someone. How did it make you feel helping out like that?

_____

_____

_____

_____

_____

_____

_____

_____

_____

_____

_____

_____

_____

_____

_____

What's the most dangerous thing in the world in your opinion?

_____

_____

_____

_____

_____

_____

_____

_____

_____

_____

_____

_____

_____

_____

_____

What celebrity do you seem to just love to hate? Why
do you?

_____

_____

_____

_____

_____

_____

_____

_____

_____

_____

_____

_____

_____

_____

Tell a short story about a hero, but from the perspective of the person he saved

_____

_____

_____

_____

_____

_____

_____

You encounter a weird and exotic creature. It performs a creepily seductive mating dance for you. Describe the creature and it's dance in as much detail as possible.

_____

_____

_____

_____

_____

_____

What is the dumbest trend you've ever partaken in?

_____

_____

_____

_____

_____

_____

_____

_____

_____

_____

_____

_____

_____

_____

_____

_____

What do you think makes a person truly intelligent?

_____

_____

_____

_____

_____

_____

_____

_____

_____

_____

_____

_____

_____

_____

Tell an original and truly terrifying campfire horror
story.

_____

_____

_____

_____

_____

_____

_____

_____

_____

_____

_____

_____

_____

_____

What's the most important thing in life for people to
know/learn in your opinion?

_____

_____

_____

_____

_____

_____

_____

_____

_____

_____

_____

_____

_____

_____

_____

What was your first dream job as a kid? Did you hit
your mark? What's your dream job now?

_____

_____

_____

_____

_____

_____

_____

_____

_____

_____

_____

_____

_____

_____

_____

_____

Imagine you stayed up for four days straight. You start to hallucinate. What do you see?

_____

_____

_____

_____

_____

_____

_____

_____

_____

_____

_____

_____

_____

_____

What's the most (not necessarily favorite) emotion-evoking song for you? Why does it make you feel the way it does? Write a few lines of it that resonate with you and explain why.

_____

_____

_____

_____

_____

_____

_____

_____

_____

_____

_____

_____

What would be the theme of this year for you? What
about the month? Week?

_____

_____

_____

_____

_____

_____

_____

_____

_____

_____

_____

_____

_____

What's the one thing you constantly procrastinate
with? Why do you put it off all the time?

_____

_____

_____

_____

_____

_____

_____

_____

_____

_____

_____

_____

_____

_____

What is it that bonds you to your significant other
or your closest friend?

_____

_____

_____

_____

_____

_____

_____

_____

_____

_____

_____

_____

_____

_____

List all the people that you wish were dead. Whether you know them personally or not. Or just list different kinds of people that need to be dead (e.g. Hipsters).

_____

_____

_____

_____

_____

_____

_____

_____

_____

_____

_____

_____

_____

_____

Write a note to Santa telling him off for not giving
you what you wanted for Christmas as a kid.

_____

_____

_____

_____

_____

_____

_____

_____

_____

_____

_____

_____

_____

Write a review of a new movie you want to see but
have just seen the trailer for.

_____

_____

_____

_____

_____

_____

_____

_____

_____

_____

_____

_____

_____

_____

_____

What are your parents like? Can you see how you are
half your mother and father (if you are)?

_____

_____

_____

_____

_____

_____

_____

_____

_____

_____

_____

_____

_____

_____

What is the most offensive thing to you? Why does it get you butthurt?

_____

_____

_____

_____

_____

_____

_____

_____

_____

_____

_____

_____

_____

_____

_____

It's been found that Ramen isn't even close to a
thing that can be called food. What is it really?

_____

_____

_____

_____

_____

_____

_____

Would you rather take a bullet for a stranger or
shoot a loved one in the fucking face? Explain.

_____

_____

_____

_____

_____

_____

_____

_____

If (or when) you retire, what do you plan to do with
your life?

_____

_____

_____

_____

_____

_____

_____

_____

_____

_____

_____

_____

_____

What's the nicest thing you ever did for a complete stranger?

_____

_____

_____

_____

_____

_____

_____

_____

_____

_____

_____

_____

_____

_____

What do you think needs to be done to leave this
world a better place for future generations?

_____

_____

_____

_____

_____

_____

_____

_____

_____

_____

_____

_____

_____

_____

_____

What kind of book/movie/comic/etc. ended too soon
that you wish was still continuing to be made?

_____

_____

_____

_____

_____

_____

_____

_____

_____

_____

_____

_____

_____

What's your favorite comic book? If you don't read
comics, wtf is wrong with you?

_____

_____

_____

_____

_____

_____

_____

"She queefed so hard that . . ."

_____

_____

_____

_____

_____

_____

_____

ABOUT THE AUTHOR

CJ Carr lives and "works" in the Metro Detroit area. He loves to read (especially comics), watch TV, listen to good tunes, and hang-out with Jamie (his BFF). He goes to school for creative writing at Oakland University and plans on writing a number of books in the very near future.

For now, you can pick up his other book, *29 Years of Nothing: A Compilation of a Schizophrenic's Half-Finished Works and Other Random Stuff.*